I0164182

Time

M.O.R.E. Publishers Corp.
St. Louis, Missouri

M.O.R.E. Publishers Corp.
P.O. Box 38285
St. Louis, MO 63138

www.MOREPublishers.com

MOREPublishersCO@AOL.com

Copyright 2006 W. A. Neal
All rights reserved.
Reproduction in whole or in part without
the expressed written permission of the
publisher is prohibited.

Printed in the United States

ISBN 978-0-9801647-5-6

PRAISE THE CHILDREN AND THEY WILL BLOSSOM.

William A. Neal II

MY BOOK IS
DEDICATED TO MY
WIFE AND CHILDREN

Table of Contents

About the Author

William Neal II, songwriter, singer, and minister, is better known for his musical talents than for his poetry. Yet the poetry that he writes follows the rhythms of emotion that are expressed throughout his music. In addition to releasing <u>Time</u>, the first published collection of his writings, Mr. Neal has produced a CD entitled <u>Love Mission</u>.

Time

For something very special,
Like blossoms in the spring;
A thousand rays of sunshine,
To make the children sing!

To smell the breakfast cooking,
The taste of water pure;
These things He did provide us,
God loves us all, I'm sure!

The ticking of the clock,
It tells us when to go;
But how do geese know when to fly,
Before the winter snow?

God's timing is in the making,
So good He's never late,
When man often fails,
When trying to create.

Do flowers know the wind will blow,
And the sun will follow soon?
Does man know without his clock
When it's afternoon?

Have you thought to praise the Lord,
For all His mighty deeds?
He's made for us the fruit and trees.
We only plant the seeds.

This clock I hear ticking,
As it hangs upon my wall,
Has finally told what time it is –
God's time. He's done it all!

Help Us to Endure
(A Husband's Words)

So many things are wonderful
Like colors in the SPRING,
The touch of your hair;
My children that you did bare.

So many things are joyful
With the master in my life;
The softness of a tender voice
in a loving wife.

So many things are respectful
Like a greeting with a smile.
If I'm asked to walk a block
I'll probably walk a mile.

So many things are helpful
In a world that's so unkind.
It helps to know you love me
With a love that's so divine.

So many things are peaceful
Like knowing, you are saved

By the might of His power
When he arose from the grave.

So many things are lawful
Like standing on God's word.
I depend on His promise
And not on what I've heard.

So many things are spiritual:
They're hidden in God's word;
His plans for the family,
For Mother, Boy and Girl.

My Father who art in Heaven
So righteous and so pure,
Please put your arms around me
And help me to endure.

God Has No Big Shot Saints

Humble me Lord when they lift me up.
Humility is what I must claim.
Teach me to honor and give you all of the glory,
And not to seek fortune, nor seek fame.

Teach me to honor your servants.
Keep peace with all of thy men.
Let no shrine be built in my image.
Let me be known as thy friend.

Help me to hate sinful pride.
Keep me from shame and disgrace,
for there are no "Big Shots" in Heaven
So fill me with mercy and grace.

The fear of the Lord is to hate evil,
Pride and arrogance do Thy hate;
So mold me, and teach me, dear Lord,
There are "No Big Shots" called "Saints."

IT DON'T MATTER

It don't matter what I say.
The Lord is gonna have His way.
You could be still and learn to wait,
Trust in God; increase your faith.

It don't matter what I say.
The Lord commanded us to pray.
Don't play the role of Jezebel –
Satan rules her very well.

It don't matter what I say.
The Lord is gonna have His way.
See Jesus died and wept for you.
Don't buy a lie. Don't sell the truth.

It don't matter what I see.
The world is not family,
And because He gave His life for us
Is why I lean upon His trust.

So what does matter, "Son of Man,"
Is that we serve the Great I Am.
He gave His life on Calvary
That we might live eternally.

Master Can

Can you build a mountain?
Can you part the sea?
Send a plague of locust
On your enemies?

Can you kill a giant,
With a rock and sling;
Will you stretch out on a cross
Between two dying thieves?

Can you build a kingdom?
Can you walk alone?
Can you feed a multitude, or
Turn someone into stone?

Can you cross a desert
With just a rod and staff?
Will you ride a donkey
While others mock and laugh?

So can you call Him Master?
Will you call him great?
He stood between those pillars
And He controls the quakes.

The Path of Life

Life is like the wind
Like the new fallen snow.
It's here for a while
And then it must go.

Life is like the ocean,
So wide and so deep.
Careful, how you cross it -
Many fall beneath.

Life is like the moon,
Shining on a hill
Showing you the shadows
Lurking in the still.

Life is but the Master
Living in our dream
Giving us a vision
Of what life really means.

Because Christ gave His life
Like the new fallen snow
Is the reason why I love Him;
And my life, I let it go.

Dare

Dare to be different.
Dare to be great.
Dare to be humble.
Dare to walk straight.

Dare to be honest.
Dare to be sweet.
Dare to be grateful.
Dare to be meek.

Dare to be skillful.
Dare to be kind.
Dare to be holy.
Dare to be mine.

Dare to be gentle.
Dare to speak soft.
I dare you to praise Him,
And carry your cross.

I dare you to love Him.
I dare you to shout,
"Jesus is Lord,
Now Satan come out!"

15

The Poor

Do you love the poor?
For there are many near and far.
Some travel by bus
And never had a car.

Some sit along the wayside
And beg a place to rest.
Some gave the poor a place to stay
To him the Lord did bless.

But do you love the poor
When you meet them on the street
Begging for a dollar
To get a bite to eat?

Surely you are blessed
So reach out for his hand.
Give him of your goods.
Say you understand.

So have you not your blessing?
For the Father has fed you good.
Have you forgot the poor,
Your love for brotherhood?

Now every knee shall bow
And every tongue confess
For I never knew you, brethren,
If the poor, you did not bless.

Luke 4:18, 19

A Soft Answer

In time of despair,
Don't you know God is there?
Let a soft answer reply.

Sometimes you feel weak
But arise to your feet.
Let a soft answer reply.

If your brother is unkind
This is when you must shine.
Let a soft answer reply.

When you feel that you are right
For this cause do we strike -
Let a soft answer reply.

So the Brethren must love,
Be gentle as doves
For the power is His from on High.

Be humble, be meek,
For we won't taste defeat:
Let a soft answer reply.

Slick

Beware of Slick
He's crafty and quick
He comes like a thief in the night

He'll walk by your side
He'll ask for a ride
He'll even sit down for a bite

He'll call you his friend
He'll come back again
And sing you a sweet lullaby

He'll come in your house
Make a pass at your spouse
And come short of just telling a lie

He'll say that he cares
In time of despair
On him you can surely depend

But remember the name
God has made it so plain
He's SLICK, disguised as your friend

The Unprofitable Servants

No servant can serve two masters
No eagle can soar without wings
No mountain will move without faith
No kingdom to build without kings.

No servant can serve two masters
No river will flow without rain
No tree will bare fruit before season
No saint can be molded without pain.

No servant can serve two masters
He will love one and hate the other
Beware of the devil's devices
He comes to accuse the brethren.

The Lord has commanded his servants
For we do unto the Lord as He commands
For we know that at the end of our journey
The unprofitable servants will stand.

My Father

A boy is the image
Of his father in his prime
Looking for answers
Racing against time.

Laughing and playing
In years they will grow,
To bond with each other
And then he must go.

His manhood will reach him
His pride and ego,
Will lead him through changes
Some high and some low.

He'll make wrong decisions
And cry in despair,
But Father is watching
His hands are still there.

Oh thanks, dear Father
For believing in me;
The best that you are
Is what I will be.

Teach Us Love

Teach us, Lord, to follow You
Help us to walk straight,
Fill us with Your Holy Spirit:
With patience, do we wait.

Teach us how to love You,
Help us to be kind,
Standing on Your precious promise
With Your love divine.

Teach us to be skilful
With our gifts that You gave
Give us strength for the journey;
We need You everyday.

Teach us to be humble
Help us to be pure;
Lead us when we're weary,
Help us to endure.

And when our journey's over
You'll open Heaven's door
To bring us closer to You
To dwell forever more.

Anger

Anger is a feeling
We must all control;
If we tame our anger
We can reach our goal.

When our brother is angry
He must learn to pray;
For the Lord has power
To take it away.

Speak soft like a songbird
Be gentle as a dove;
Be firm with your answer
But rooted in love.

Be quick to the hearing
And slow when you speak;
Be given to fasting
Be chaste and discrete.

For anger may kindle
A great flame of fire,

A smokescreen of vengeance
With evil desires.

But Jesus is faithful
In Him, we can trust:
For all that obey Him
He's faithful and just.

So when anger is present
And you're full of rage,
Remember to call Jesus:
In Him, we are saved.

www.ingramcontent.com/pod-product-compliance
Lightning Source LLC
Chambersburg PA
CBHW030013040426
42337CB00012BA/764